Tree Stand Scribbles

Tom Yarbrough

RIVER HAWK BOOKS
ADA, OKLAHOMA

Tree Stand Scribbles

©2012 Tom Yarbrough. All rights reserved.

ISBN: 78-0-615-69466-5

Order from Amazon.com or Lulu.com.

Discount available when ordered in bulk quantities. For more information, contact

River Hawks Books   P.O. Box 381   Ada, OK 74820

Visit our website at
https://sites.google.com/site/tomyarbroughwritings/

All rights reserved. No part of this book may be reproduced, transmitted, or stored in whole or in part by any means without permission in writing from the author and the publisher. Except in the brief case of brief quotations embodied in critical articles and reviews.

Cover photo by arrangement Bonita R. Cheshier via Shutterstock.

My Thanks to:

Jodie and Georgianna Eiland for excellent hunting land.

Brother Gene Yarbrough for years of kind support.

Sons Tom E. and John Yarbrough for their art works.

Grandsons Jason, Chris, Zack, and John Tyler for their youth and energy.

All the guys above helped build our cabin in the woods and suffered through my first Sayings.

And of course, much thanks to my wife, Trisha, who remains strong encouragement through all my shotgun writings.

The Start

One fall evening I **stumbled** back into deer camp.

My brother, sons and grandsons jumped to me, "*Are you hurt?*"

"*No, just tired.*" Then I grinned and drew from my pocket a crumpled piece of paper.

On it, I'd **scribbled**:

> Up in my tree stand
> Feeling disappointment.
> Began feeling grand.
> Why can't the deer,
> Keep my appointment?

After, they guffawed, "*But did you see any deer?*"

I saw no deer that day. But it started me 20 years of writing <u>Tree Stand Scribbles</u>.

I intend to give you a little **chuckle** in a sometimes dreary world.

I offer these sayings as an adventure with humor. I hope this work shoots an arrow at you old hunters and new alike.

Have a **laugh** on me!

Me

Deer fat and sassy,
  Sneaking from tree to tree.
  Kinda reminds me of me.

Cookies

My wife may complain
Of my hunt in the wood.
But from the beginning
She knew where I stood.
She smiles, puts her hands
On her hips,
And bakes me some chocolate chips.

Armadillo

Armadillo
Tough as brillo
Among the leaves.
Invading my space
Like in a race
Hurry, hurry
Could be late.
Did not count on my 38.

Woodsy Instincts!

What has great legs?
Can see like a hawk,
Knows how to stalk;
And can smell you a mile away?
Your wife!

Buck Fever

Buck fever in the morning,
Buck fever in the night,
Was I just snoring?
It's a doe day all right.

Raccoon

A raccoon grunted
Under my stand today,
I could not scare him away.
I thought he was a pig
while he did his jig.

Up a tree, next to me, he went.
Stared at me like I should pay rent.
So I asked Mr. Coon,

If he'd seen any deer.

He said, "Some quite near."

But I said, *where, I can't see!*

Coon said, "Why not, dummy,

You're up **in my tree."**

Rut

During Rut
Deer get dumb,
Like some people's brains,
Just plain numb.
But since in the rutting,
Deer do get dumb,
I think I'll go get me some.

One Thing

One thing a deer can do that a human can't: Take a dump while running.

One thing a human can do a deer can't: Read a magazine while dumping.

A Good Decoy

My grandson placed a decoy deer,
Beneath his stand so near,
His cousin surprised with bugging eyes
Nearly shot it in the rear.

Wrong food

Better be careful,
On a tree stand hunt.
Too many sweet potatoes
Surprise you with a grunt.

Good Wind

Expel air in your bunk,
Lingers like a skunk.
Expel air in your stand,
Nature's wind
Stays your friend.

Female Coyote

Ms Coyote roamed
And dug under my stand.
She looked as if to stay.
With a "whoosh"
I shooed her away.
This was her lucky day.

Apple Pieces

Cut apple pieces
Thrown down for deer,
Scrubby coyote ate them
Purrrty near.
Strange mysterious world
Who gets food.

?? **One View** ??
Men like to hunt.
Women like to shop.
To be very blunt,
The MALL costs a lot!

Been There

You reading this,
You've been there
Up in a deer stand,
Floating in the air.

Messages

My oldest son shot a big buck.
<u>Phone texts began</u>:
Youngest to oldest son:
"*Did you shoot?*"
Oldest: "*Shot a big one.*"
Youngest: "*Did you get him?*"
Oldest: "*Shot a big one.*"
Youngest: "*Do you need help?*"
Oldest: "*Lost the blood trail.*"
Youngest: "*Do you need help?*"
Oldest: "*Need some better eyes.*"
<u>Grandson chimed in</u>:
"*No, you need a better shot!*"

[Team search got the deer.]

Happy

Writing sayings in a tree,
Happy as can be;
Family back at fireside
Laughing straight at me

Time

One son killed a buck.
A grandson killed a doe.
Other son bagged a doe.
Another grandson got a buck.
My brother and I killed some time.

Perspective 1

Some people say,
Hunting deer is so savage,
But many hunters miss,
Suggests the national average.

Perspective 2

Some see deer
as magnificent beast,
Fried eggs and tenderloin
Make a wonderful feast!

Unlucky Buck!

Hunter's luck.
Unlucky buck.

Sounds in the Woods

The owl persists with pulsing hoot.
Coyote yelps its hungry heart,
Crow gives caw to group it up.
Deer keep silent from the start.

What sounds do men make?
Crash, bang, yell, crack, smash,
Snore, cry, laugh, then fart.

Confused

How can I stand
This freezing wind?
Hey, sun's coming out,
Ain't life grand?

Daydreaming

If you're in a tree stand,
Thinking about your pension,
You may be grand,
But you've lost your attention.

Wild Dog

Shot a wild dog,
In November fog;
He sickly chased deer.
Threw him one handed,
In a deep ditch stranded.
         My mind was 30.
         My arm was 70.
         Right elbow popped,
Made me left-handed.

Wild Dogs Running

         Some days you just
         don't want to shoot
         anything.
A kind of peace lulls the hunt.
    You just enjoy
whatever Nature brings,
Then the wild dogs pull their stunt.
    Should I shoot them?
      Or let them go?
    My head says, "Yes!"
    My heart says, "No."

Squirrel Dance

A female squirrel runs from a male.
She darts left and right then stops.
She wants him to chase her.
She flicks her tail
 with a beckoning call,
As if to say,
"That ain't all."
 "I can out run you, buster,
With all your male luster."

Smell

Up in a tree stand,
I sat thoughtfully.

I whiffed something rank.
Was it skunk, bear, or deer?

Radiating week-old stank,
The smell was me!

The Coat

One grandson forgot his coat on
opening day.
He shrugged and said,
"What can I say?"
I loaned him a coat
for the cold, windy morn.
Sometimes grandsons cause pain
like a thorn,
I'm still **so** grateful they were born.

Surprise

Up in my tree,
On a limb so slim. I glanced:
A buck looked straight at me.
        I blinked.
        He winked.
Last I saw of him.

The Rat

There stood an old shed
By a new cabin fair.
Each day a rat
Moved from its lair.

We sat by the fire
And watched it outwit us,
Til Jason with cheese
Did finally redeem us.

The trap went slap.
The rat went splat.

Pictures were taken
As history was making
And THAT was THAT.

Coyote Family

One evening by the campfire,
Coyotes bayed louder than
Our fireside talk.
See, Mama returned
from a long Hunting stalk.

We thought of family
As we looked at each other,
Remembering what it felt to
Know a caring mother.

Oklahoma Wind

Wind gusts,
Wind puffs,
Wind seems gruff,
Wind stays tough.
Deer don't like it.

Looking at a Salt Block

Staring at a salt block,
Moving toward depression,
Wondering where the deer are
During this writing session.

Freezers

Acorns dropping in
crisp brown leaves
Announce the change
of singing oak trees.
They tell the story of coming cold.
Acorns make deer slightly bold.
Hunters listen to turning nature.
Some freezers get full
beyond all reason.
Others remain empty
for another season.

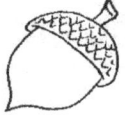

Do They Know?

Do the deer know we're here?
It isn't perfectly clear.

Camp Joke

<u>Made-up joke
from my oldest grandson:</u>
*You know why deer go to a doctor?
---To get a buck shot!*

Part Blind

Squirrels keep strolling,
Fog still rolling,
Can't see deer anyway.

Cobwebs

Cobwebs sparkle
in morning sun,
I'm in a tree stand,
having more fun.
> Spider spins a web,
> Could break any day.
> I just dream of bed
> But hunt any way.

False Alarm

> Dead branch crashing,
> Wakes me from a stare.
> Adrenalin pumping;
> Heart a-jumping;
> Deer aren't anywhere.

Safer in Tree Stand

In a tree stand,
Being one with Nature,
Sitting still is grand.
Some say safer.

To Stop a Deer

A deer runs by fast,
Whistle to make him stop.
Soon my trusty rifle
Signals with a "pop."

Home Thoughts

Shivering and cold to the bone,
Makes you think of recliner at home.
Some might say I'm just plain lazy,
That kind of thinking remains
quite hazy.
Stay-at-home folks think I'm just
plain crazy.

Some Say

My wife will bury me in the woods,
Under my tree stand, with my
hunting rifle.
They say that way she'll always
know where I am.

November Hunt

So cold,
Very bold,
Feeling old
Then it's hot.
Reminds me of deer stew
Cooking in the pot.

SLEEPY
Even in a tree stand
Nodding
Up and down,
Back and forth
All around,
Sleep still tempts me. **zzzzz**

Old Timer

A strange stillness
covers the wood,
Like a blanket hood,
Old timers will say,
That's a deery day!

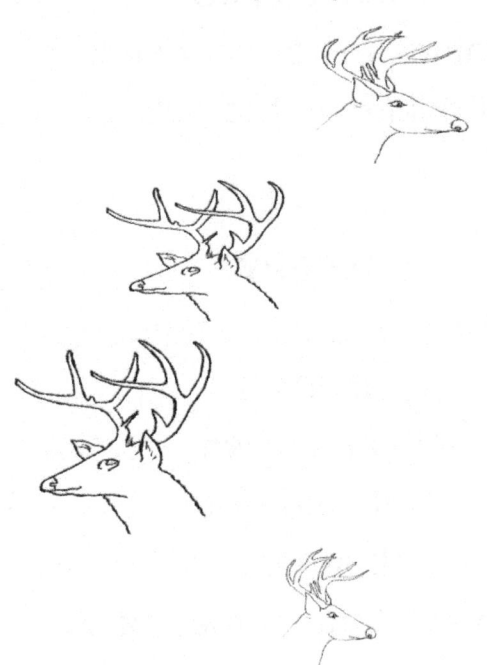

Gold

Tree stand, tree stand,
You are mighty old.
But seeing deer first,
You're like pure gold.

Wise Geese

I saw some geese fly South,
Honking all the way,
While deer, coon, and coyote are
Seen in town any day,
I'm glad to see geese
Remember Nature's way.

Scribbling in a Tree Stand

Sitting in a tree stand,
Looking with one eye.
Writing cramps my hand,
As all the deer sneak by.

From Mouths of Babes

One of my grandsons, aged 5, prayed at Thanksgiving dinner:
"Dear Lord, thank you granddad got a deer on his hunt."

I had not been hunting yet.
You may wonder:
Did I get a deer
later that day?
Actually, I **did**.

Early Rabbit

Just before daylight,
In the middle of the road,
A rabbit sat.
The headlights confused him,
He ran this way and that.
I'm sure he was pleased,
The gas pedal I eased
So not to cause a big splat!

Atmosphere

Wet leaves,
Soft as pillows.
Wet trees,
Weep like willows.
Sitting in a tree,
Wet as can be.
Should I stay,
Marvel at Nature's way?
Deer don't care.
At home anywhere.

Spent Hours

5000 hours in a deer stand;
Some think that's sad.
Can't get them back.
Like I'd been had.
Just as well been there,
As sleeping in the sack.

Tough Mosquitoes

Mosquitoes sensing the heat,
Gathering for a blood letting.
Eerie buzzing around head net,
Abruptly stopping to inspect.
Can't get through.
Buzz again.
Find the hole.
Poke it out.
Fifteen bites across your back.
Arms aren't made to do the whack.
Sitting on a deer stand,
Mosquitoes know
You're the rack.

ON OUR TREE STANDS WE MAY
WORSHIP NATURE. AND
GUESS WHAT?
NATURE WORSHIPS US BACK!

Mighty Oak

Too many oak trees,
Nature's little joke.
Is it Burr, Blackjack, or Post-oak?
White or Red?
Live or Dead?

As many trees as kinds of people,
Can they stand like
Oak's strong steeple?

My Old Stand

When I was gone,
Lightning hit my stand.
I lost an old friend,
Crumpled and gnarled.

My old friend stood twisted.
Lightning did the do,
Even though he resisted.
Nature may be stronger,
Bolts like a bomber

He said, "*build me anew.*"
"*I have the best view--*
"*I have the best reason.*"

Twenty year old stand,
Good for another season.

Two Trees Kissing

Two trees kissing,
Leaning over a deer trail.
One tree rubbed by
a well-loved rack,
One tree rubbed by
a female's back.
Female's scent rubbed
as it stands.
Other tree rubbed by
anxious male glands.

When You Miss a Buck

When you miss a buck,
You shoulda oughta got,
You feel like a drunken sot.

Breathing hard,
Wasn't your card.
Eyes cross-eyed,
Thought you'd died,

One free buck makes it so.
One clear miss
Have to watch him go,

Where's that luscious doe again?

GET READY

Wasps flying tall,
Having a ball.
Male squirrels twirl,
Looking for a girl.
I look at my hand,
Hearing Nature's band.
Better get ready,
Deer under my stand.

Haunted

For some,
Hunters' possession
Becomes the
Session of obsession.

Focus

Focus, focus, focus.
Be at the right place,
At the right time.
Don't depend on
Hocus pocus.

Early morning

Early morning sunrise
In a tree stand,
Why does the sun,
Keep poking at my eyes?

Deer Cycle

Know the cycle:

Misjudge.

Find the cycle.

Get in sludge.

Work the cycle.

Out there late.

Miss the cycle.

Empty plate.

Deer gone.

One with Nature

When in the woods, sitting in a tree,
there is a moment when stillness
overtakes the body.

Your body starts to
hum with the pulse
of your natural surroundings.
All your senses become energized
so you feel blended, at least,
at one with Nature.
The moment lasts only
a little while but you sense
that this is much like
being pure spirit without a body.
The deer remain perplexed
because you appear

                Invisible.

Ground Blind

Sitting in a ground blind
Makes it hard to swivel.
Raking leaves with your feet,
Sounds like rainy drizzle.

WEATHER

Weather changing,
Re-arranging,
Wind's a blowing,
Limbs go crashing.
Glad it's not snowing.

Getting Ready Again

Ready for deer hunt wholehearted,
Seems to be over,

And just got started.

Weather Changes

Sweating, freezing
Hate that sneezing!

Nose

Sitting in a deer stand,
Cold wind blowing.
Looks like could be snowing.
Nose a-running,
But really can't spit,
Where is a tissue,
When you most need it?

Alert

Bushes rattling,
Deer alert.
Bad shooting day,
They won't get hurt.

Wind Factor

Wind North by Northwest,
Deer can't smell me.
Bucks still know best;
Me, to some degree.
Oops- - - just saw one flee!

Hunger

Up in a tree,
Stomach growling.
Eat a pecan,
May slow hunger.
Sure not getting any younger!

A Kiss

Trees protruding out of ground
like magnified whiskers,
Some stretching left,
some stretching right,
All try to kiss rays of sunlight.
Trees feel a kind of bliss.
People stay like the trees,
Reaching this way and that
On their knees,
Hoping for a kiss.

Don't Give Up

Your deer hunting view
Need not be skewed
By reading these ditties so true.
So one day when you're blue,
And you haven't got a clue,
Take a look at these,
For some funny ease.
I may not be Shakespeare,
But put it in gear.
Hunting is still very near.

One Less Coyote

I used to say I ate what I shot.
Sometimes life changes—or not.
Once, coyote scared deer away.
One less coyote that bright day.
Mangy, trotting through woods
hurry, hurry.
He did not bank on my 30—30.

RAIN

In a tree stand
Rain seems an oddity.
But as drinking water,
It's a commodity.

Missed !

Missed the shot.
What have I bought?

Opening Deer Day

When viewing outside time and space,
My mind travels to the woods,
Where owls hoot, coyotes yelp, squirrels pace, and
Deer can freeze time as they should.
There sounds a sonata in the woods.

The insects, the trees, the animals,
The southeast wind play it best.
No man-made instrument tells it so,
Only a mystical warble,
When time stands at rest.

Early Oct. Morn

A tree kissed me on the head today.
No . . . I did not bump my head.
It was a natural thing.
Fall had come,
Wind did run
Sun had fun.
October gave her sign in full,
An old rotten twig fell on my skull,
As I penned this awkward rhyme.

Heaven

Some say I'd go hunting if I were on my death bed.   I might go to heaven instead.

Hair

Beard,
    Gray and long.
        Growing, stroking, flowing.
      I like it still.
        Feel it!

Sun

Sun's a rising,
Shadows on the grass.
Leaves turn golden,
Like shiny brass.
Pay close attention,
Deer are coming.
Quit that daydreaming,
And stop that Sunning.

Ms. Hawk

A female hawk soars proudly
through the air.
On rapid currents she's so fair.
But she does not have an easy life,
'Cause under her feathers,
Work fleas, ticks and lice
To pester her daily strife.
They're often like people
who cut like a knife.

Hunting Knife

Admiring a hunting knife,
By talented Jim Sasser.
Daylight drawing near.
Better hurry along,
Instead of looking at gear.
Move to my deer stand,
Much, much faster.

Nursery Rhyme

Jack and Jill went up the hill,
holding hand and hand.
On windy days,
I grab a branch,
Swaying with the
'ol tree stand.

Burst of Joy

While sitting in a tree stand,
A burst of joy
Seems to signal
Unlimited creativity.

North Wind

Wind from the North
Smells like marsh.
Are the deer very near?
The wind blows harsh.

North wind sways a tree
With a mighty force.
Do the deer ever think
I'm the source?
One thing's clear,
Gonna make me hoarse.

Fog

Foggy day,
Trees weep like rain.
Deer still play,
Ignore any pain.

Baseball Memory

Falling leaves,
Beneath the trees,
From Nature's stem
Did send them.

The time of year flows in between,
life and love that I have seen;
Reflections on the past
Make futures seem obscene.

Squirrels throw nuts like a curve,
Upon the earth they swerve.
No baseball pitcher does it better.

Thanksgiving Day

Up in a tree
on Thanksgiving day,
You have to stop
to eat some dinner.
But in my heart I want to stay.
Wife says,
"Don't be a beginner,
Come eat!
You're still a winner."

Late Leaves

Sitting in a tree stand,
Rifle on my knee.
Left hand on the forearm,
Right on the safety.
Too many leaves today.
Hard to really see.

Anticipation

Bright morning--

so clear.

Have no fear.

Harvest your deer.

Rhyme

Hunter poems
should sorta rhyme,
If they're worth a dime!

Chair Mirrors

I'm going to invent some
side mirrors
For my tree chair.
Deer sneak behind me.
Always know I'm there.
[*Somebody probably already has.*]

A Bee

A bee kissed me on the cheek today.
He was just friendly,
But I shooed him away,
      Anyway!

DANGER

Leaves so green and yellow,
Look to be so mellow,
But look under the leaves instead
To spy Mister Copper . . . Head.

Chipmunk

Chipmunk, chipmunk
Like Chip and Dale.
You flash about,
Make others look pale.
You seem so fast beyond
all creatures,
Better watch for the
red-hawk features.

Wind Damaged Tree

Silhouetted against the sunrise,
Bent a three inch rounded oak.
The base stood mostly rotted,
Wind-torn and besotted.

It groaned and cracked,
Moaned and racked,
But wanted to stay alive.

Across a deep deer path,
A tall brother stopped wind's wrath.
The little oak would not break.
Brother branches like arms,
Embraced him in his wake.

Early Fall

Fresh fallen leaves,
Southern Fall breeze,
Downwind from deer,
You know they're near.

Hunter Staring at Rocks

Instead of looking at my socks,
I stared at deserted rocks.

Edges, protruding angles,
A shapely shadow mocks.

For in those crevices,
Hides the life of ages:
A plant grows

From old parent sages.

Warming Hands

In a deer stand,
Warming shooting hand,
North wind's a killer,
Wish it'd get stiller.

North Wind Again

North wind does not blend,
East or West or South.
    Eyes watering,
    Ears aching,
    Very dry mouth.
Wind blows here and there,
Spirals like a steeple,
Puffs up mysteriously,
Just like some people.

Usual Nature

Crunching **noise** behind me,
Swiveled in my seat,
Startled,
what did I see?
Happy usual Nature
peeking back at me.

Autumn Leaves

Some spin over and over,
Like a bicycle pedal.
Some float back and forth,
Before they want to settle.
Some sway with the breeze
Like a kite.
Autumn leaves,
What a sight!

Dew Doubt

Drop, drop, drop,
Dew from trees,
Percussion symphony.
Two deer paths converge
Below my knees.
One heads east,
One heads west,
I don't know
Which one's best.

Two chances of life
Converge my mind.
One leads left,
One leads right.
Times I wish I had
Second sight.

Perhaps the way
Shows clear in knowing,
But I sit here
Doubts ever showing.

Keys

<u>Turn one simple key.</u>
<u>Whole new worlds:</u>

Lock to the mind's eye.
Lock to a house.
Lock to a business.
Lock to a school.
Lock to an auto.
Lock to a safe
Lock to a pasture gate.
Lock to a gun cabinet.

One Word

Some single words create sayings:

Camping.

Dreaming.

Inventing.

Spatula.

Tarantula.

Hunting.

Baseball and Nature

The times of year,
Flow in between,
The baseball games
I **would** have seen.

Missed Games

The time of year flows
in between,
The baseball games
I **could** have seen.

Fresh Snow

Fresh snow in the woods glistens,
Like pure white glaze, the icing listens.
The icicles form the decorated ferns.
Her tears drop like melting burns
Sometimes snow stays charming,
But, sitting in a tree stand,
Cold on my back grows

alarming.

Repeats

If any of these sayings

I did repeat,

It's only because of

My numb, dumb seat!

But remember,

Poems are like water and ice.

Reading once may not suffice.

Quitting the hunt

Stopping the hunt
Is like losing a friend,
But the deer
Don't think so
At the very end.

Last Day Deer Hunt

Last Day.   Break away.
Who can say?
Last Day.
Stay awhile.   Make do.
Blessings flow.
Who can know?
Powers that be.
Up in a tree.
See a long way off.
No matter
Deer scatter.

OOPS!

Text-messaging my sweetheart
From my tree stand,
Appears a deer with a start,
Bumped the tree with my hand.
No good stand!!
Come on deer,
Have a heart!

Made in the USA
Monee, IL
27 September 2023